Alexander the Great

by William Caper

Table of Contents

Introduction

Thousands of years ago, a boy named Alexander grew up to become a great soldier. He led his army into history. Today we know him as Alexander the Great.

Alexander won every war that he fought. But he treated his enemies with honor and respect. Though he was successful in war, he wanted to bring people together to live in peace.

In this book you will learn about the life and achievements of Alexander the Great. As you read, think about what it was like to live in Alexander's time.

Alexander founded more than seventy cities. His **empire** (EHM-pigh'r) stretched from Greece to Egypt to the Near East. After he died, a new age of learning, science, and art swept through the empire he left behind.

Alexander's Early Life

356 B.C.–338 B.C.

Thousands of years ago, Greece was one of the most advanced **civilizations** (sih-vih-lih-ZAY-shuns) in the world. But a kingdom to the north slowly grew stronger. This kingdom was Macedonia (ma-seh-DOH-nee-uh). Its king was Philip II. In 356 B.C., Philip and his wife Olympias had a son. They named him Alexander.

According to legend, Alexander's mother was related to Achilles, the mythical hero of the Trojan War. Philip was said to be descended from Hercules, a Greek hero known for his strength. Hercules was the son of Zeus.

This map shows Macedonia and Greece. Can you find Pella, in the center of Macedonia? Alexander was born there.

ALEXANDER'S FIRST CONQUEST

When Alexander was about twelve, his father was offered a handsome, powerful horse. But no one could tame it.

Alexander said he could tame it. Alexander saw that the horse was afraid of his shadow. He turned the horse so he could not see his shadow. He spoke to the horse gently, then leaped on its back and rode off!

Philip gave the horse to Alexander, who named it Bucephalus (byoo-SEH-fuh luhs). The name means "ox-head." Bucephalus had a large head and big eyes: like an ox.

PRIMARY SOURCE

A Proud Father

The scholar Plutarch wrote a book about Alexander. Plutarch described how Alexander tamed the horse Bucephalus when his father could not. When Alexander got up on the horse, his proud father said, "O my son, look thee out a kingdom equal and worthy to thyself, for Macedonia is too little for thee."

ALEXANDER'S EDUCATION

King Philip wanted his son to have a good education. When Alexander was thirteen, Philip called for the Greek teacher Aristotle (A-rih-STAH-tuhl) to come teach his son. Aristotle was known as one of the greatest thinkers of his time.

Aristotle taught young Alexander about plants and animals, people and places. They talked about art, war, and many other interesting subjects.

THEY MADE A DIFFERENCE

Aristotle was a science pioneer. He spent much of his life studying animals and recording his observations. He figured out a system of grouping them according to certain traits they share. You know the system as **classification** (klas-ih-fi-KAY-shuhn). It is still used today.

By the time Alexander was sixteen, he was helping his father rule his kingdom. Philip wanted to rule western Asia, eastern Europe, and northern Africa. Once when Philip was away, people in one of the **colonies** (KAH-luh-neez) began to revolt. They didn't like their king. Alexander marched troops to the colony. He attacked its largest city and stopped the revolt.

▲ This is a statue of Alexander's father, Philip.

▲ This carving shows Alexander with his mother, Olympias.

Alexander's Conquests
338 B.C.–323 B.C.

I n 338 B.C., Philip traveled to Greece. His army fought the Greeks at Chaeronea (ker-oh-NEE-uh). Alexander led a charge. He was the first soldier to break through the Greek lines. Philip's army won the battle, and Greece fell under Philip's control.

In the East was the great empire of Persia (PER-zhuh). Years earlier, Persia had taken part of the Greek territory. Now Philip wanted it back. But he was killed before he had a chance to do so.

At twenty, Alexander became king of Macedonia. He called himself Alexander the Great.

This map shows Macedonia, Greece, and part of the Persian empire. Can you find Chaeronea, in the center of Greece?

ALEXANDER INVADES PERSIA

Alexander carried out his father's plan. In 334 B.C., he led an army into Persian territory. The Persians waited for him at the Granicus (grah-NIGH-kuhs) River, in what is now Turkey.

Alexander won the battle. But the ruler of the Persian empire, Darius (da-RIGH-uhs) III, fled before the fighting was over. Alexander would ride thousands of miles to try to capture Darius.

1. SOLVE THIS

Alexander arrived in Asia with about 14,000 Macedonian soldiers and about 7,000 Greek soldiers. In Alexander's army, what was the ratio of Macedonians to Greeks?

MATH ✓ POINT

What steps did you take to solve the problem?

▲ This picture shows the Battle of Granicus.

Alexander went south to the city of Gordium (GAWR-dee-ehm), in what is today central Turkey.

According to legend, there was in the city a wagon with a rope tied in a large, tight knot. A **prophecy** (PRAH-fih-see) said that whoever untied this knot would rule all of Asia.

Alexander tried to untie the knot. But he could not do it. Finally, he raised his sword and cut the knot with one stroke. Would the prophecy, or prediction, one day come true?

Alexander's next battle against the Persian emperor Darius was at Issus (EYE-suhs). Alexander won, but Darius fled again.

Next, Alexander captured the city of Tyre (TIGHR) in what is today Lebanon. The people welcomed him. They were happy to be freed from Persian rule.

▲ **The knot Alexander cut is called the Gordian knot.**

HISTORICAL PERSPECTIVE

Alexander is still thought of as one of the greatest military commanders in history. He was known for his use of huge siege machines. He used **catapults** (KA-tah-puhltz), mobile towers, and battering rams. Those war machines are no longer used today. Today's weapons can harm many more people over a much shorter period of time.

At Tyre, Alexander used a catapult, one of many new war machines. It could hurl heavy objects, like boulders, at walls and buildings.

MYTH OR REALITY?

DARIUS ASKS FOR PEACE

When Alexander was attacking Tyre, Darius offered money and part of his empire in return for peace. One of Alexander's generals, Parmenio (par-MEE-nee-oh), said, "I would accept if I were Alexander." Alexander said, "So would I, if I were Parmenio. But I am Alexander." Did Parmenio and Alexander really say this? We can't know for sure.

ALEXANDER ENTERS EGYPT

After capturing Tyre, Alexander marched into Egypt. There he built hismost famous city—Alexandria (A-lig-ZAN-dree-uh). He wanted Alexandria to be the new capital of his empire.

In 332 B.C., he chose a piece of land near the Nile River. He planned the city very carefully. The streets were laid out in a grid. The network of evenly spaced streets allowed cool north winds to come through.

Alexandria grew quickly and became a busy seaport.

SCALE OF MILES
0   200   400
Black Sea
MACEDONIA
BITHYNIA
Pella
GALATIA
AETOLIA
ATTALID
ACHAEA   Athens
CAPPADOCIA
RHODES   CILICIA
CRETE
Mediterranean Sea
Tyre
Alexandria

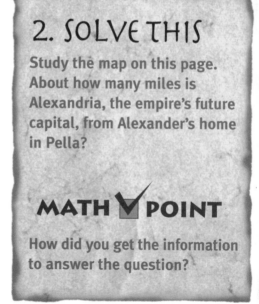

2. SOLVE THIS

Study the map on this page. About how many miles is Alexandria, the empire's future capital, from Alexander's home in Pella?

MATH ✔ POINT

How did you get the information to answer the question?

ALEXANDER BECOMES KING OF ASIA

In 331 B.C., Alexander left Egypt. He wanted to defeat Darius. Their armies met near the town of Gaugamela (gaw-guh-MEE-luh), in what is now northern Iraq.

Darius escaped a third time. Before Alexander could find him again, Darius was killed by his own soldiers.

Alexander was now the king of Asia. The prophecy of the Gordian knot had come true!

▲ Alexander finds the body of Darius.

ALEXANDER LOSES BUCEPHALUS

Alexander next traveled east to what is today Pakistan. There, he fought a powerful king, Porus (POH-ruhs), and his army. This army had 200 elephants. Alexander's men had never fought an army that included elephants.

Alexander won the battle. But his horse Bucephalus was badly wounded and later died. Alexander ordered a city built and named it Bucephala (byoo-seh-FAH-lah), in honor of the horse that had bravely carried him so far.

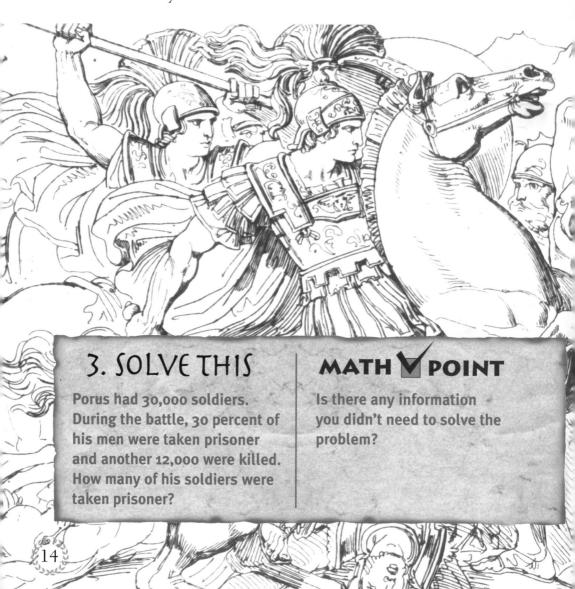

3. SOLVE THIS

Porus had 30,000 soldiers. During the battle, 30 percent of his men were taken prisoner and another 12,000 were killed. How many of his soldiers were taken prisoner?

MATH ✓ POINT

Is there any information you didn't need to solve the problem?

Alexander wanted to conquer new lands. But by now his soldiers had traveled almost 11,000 miles (18,000 kilometers). They were tired of war. They missed their homes and families. They convinced Alexander to turn back.

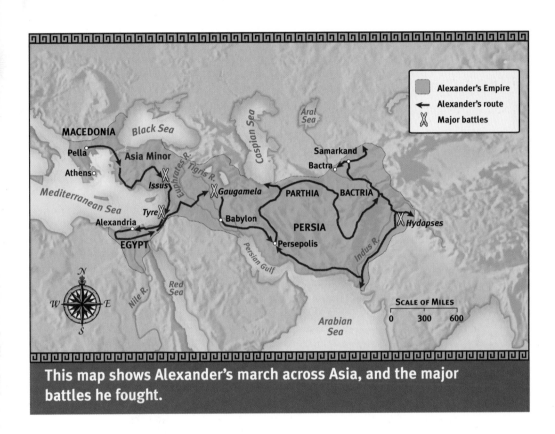

This map shows Alexander's march across Asia, and the major battles he fought.

4. SOLVE THIS

Look at the map on this page. What is the distance in miles between Gaugamela and Hydaspes?

MATH ✔ POINT

What information from the map did you use to solve the problem?

ALEXANDER'S REIGN ENDS

By 324 B.C., Alexander was king of the known world. His empire stretched from Greece in the west, to the Indus River in the east. He was ready to go home to Alexandria.

WHAT DROVE ALEXANDER?

Some people have said that Alexander was driven by a desire that in Greek is called pothos (POH-thohs). This word means a longing, or strong desire, for something that might not be possible to achieve.

Alexander returns from his conquests.

ALEXANDER DIES

Alexander wanted his empire to be one big, peaceful country. But he did not live long enough to make this happen. In 323 B.C., he fell ill with a fever. He grew weaker and weaker. In June, Alexander the Great died. He was almost thirty-three years old. His body was put in a gold sarcophagus and taken to Egypt.

the death of Alexander the Great ▲

WHERE IS ALEXANDER'S TOMB?

Hundreds of years after Alexander was buried, a king dug up his tomb. He melted the gold sarcophagus to make coins. By A.D. 300, no one knew where the tomb was. Over the years, people claimed to have found it, but where Alexander is buried remains a mystery.

☑**POINT**

Reread Chapter 2. What do you think made Alexander such a successful general?

The Hellenistic Age

323 B.C.–30 B.C.

After Alexander's death, his three top generals ruled different parts of his empire. They fought one another, but none of them was as strong as Alexander. His vast empire was no longer whole.

Like his father, Alexander had admired Greek ideas. He helped spread Greek culture throughout his empire.

The time after Alexander's death became known as the Hellenistic Age (heh-leh-NIH-stik AYJ). The word *Hellenistic* comes from the word *Hellene* (HEL-een). This was the Greek word for the Greek people. Greek culture shaped most of the known world for hundreds of years to come.

This was a time of great learning in math and science. Art became more lifelike. Philosophers suggested new ways to think about the world.

The Hellenistic Age ended when the Romans conquered the territory that had been ruled by Alexander's generals.

5. SOLVE THIS

How long did the Hellenistic Age last?

MATH ✔ POINT

What information did you need to solve the problem? Where did you find it?

▲ This statue is from the Hellenistic Age.

ALEXANDRIA

Alexander built many cities named Alexandria. The most famous was the city in Egypt near the Mediterranean Sea.

In earlier times, Athens was the center of Greek civilization. During the Hellenistic Age, Alexandria became a center of culture, trade, and learning.

Alexandria was famous for its huge museum with its gardens and courtyards. Alexandria's library was the biggest in the world. The city's rulers wanted it to store copies of all the books in the world.

IT'S A FACT

Ships arriving in Alexandria were searched for books. When books were found, they were copied for the library.

▲ This picture shows Alexandria's famous library. The "books" of this time were long sheets of paper wound in a scroll.

Alexandria's lighthouse is one of the Seven Wonders of the Ancient World. It was the height of a forty-story building, and it is the tallest lighthouse ever built.

◀ This picture shows an artist's idea of what Alexandria's famous lighthouse might have looked like.

6. SOLVE THIS

Part of the lighthouse was a regular octagon (AWK-tah-gawn) that measured about sixty feet on each side. What was the perimeter of this octagon?

MATH ✔ POINT

Explain how you solved the problem.

ECONOMY

During the Hellenistic Age, the **economy** (ee-KON-uh-mee) of the Mediterranean region grew. This happened for many reasons.

When Alexander conquered Persia, he captured large amounts of gold and silver. This money was later used for business and trade.

Each of the countries in Alexander's empire used different money. Alexander created new coins that everyone could use. This made trading easier.

Because of Alexander's conquests, new trade **routes** (ROOTS) opened. Trade went on among China, other parts of Asia, and other places to the west.

Hellenistic coins featured Alexander the Great.

GOVERNMENT

Alexander's conquests led to changes in government. Before Alexander, Greece had many **city-states** (SIT-ee-staytz). Each city-state was like a separate country.

During the Hellenistic Age, city-states fell under the control of a king who ruled a larger region. That made city-states more like cities as we know them today.

NEW GOVERNMENTS LEAD TO NEW IDEAS

When city-states were strong, people who lived in them felt safe. People explored and welcomed new ideas about life and the world.

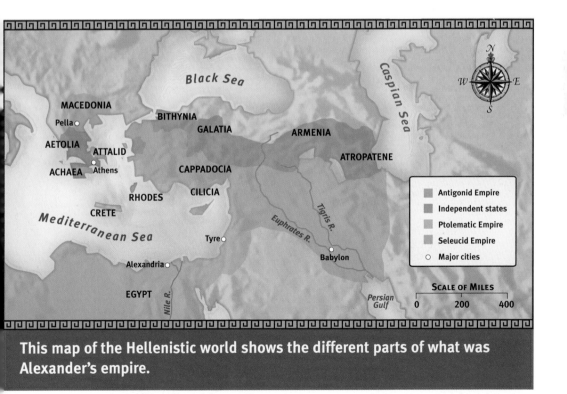

This map of the Hellenistic world shows the different parts of what was Alexander's empire.

THEY MADE A DIFFERENCE

EUCLID AND ERATOSTHENES

New ideas in mathematics were discovered in the Hellenistic Age. A Greek named Euclid (YOO-klihd) developed the ideas that led to geometry. Euclid has been called the father of geometry.

Another Greek, Eratosthenes (ehr-uh-TAHS-thuh-neez), figured out the circumference of Earth.

Euclid is called the father ▲ of geometry.

SCIENCE

Many advances in science occurred during the Hellenistic Age. Archimedes (ar-kuh-MEE-deez) invented a way to move heavy weights and large objects. If you have ever played on a see-saw, you have used a lever (LEH-ver). It is a simple machine, a bar that rests on a fixed point called a fulcrum (FUL-kruhm).

ARCHIMEDES.

A CONFIDENT SCIENTIST

According to a Greek writer, Archimedes said, "Give me a place to stand, and I will move the earth."

HARTWELL SC.

ART

Early sculptors made statues of people who looked perfect and showed little emotion. In the Hellenistic Age, statues became more lifelike. Statues showed people in action and expressing feelings. One statue of a boxer showed a very tired man with a broken nose.

This is a famous Hellenistic statue. Notice how lifelike it is. What emotions do you see in the face?

PHILOSOPHY

Philosophers from the Hellenistic Age introduced new ways to think about life. Here is what some of them said:

- Stoics (STOH-iks) are people who accept whatever happens to them and do not complain.
- Epicureans (eh-pih-KYOO-ree-ens) are people who seek simple pleasures and avoid things that cause pain.
- Cynics (SIH-niks) believe that people should ignore society's rules and live according to nature.
- Skeptics (SKEHP-tihks) are people who can't know things for certain, so they act according to how they think things appear.

Epicurus believed that seeking pleasure would make people happy.

Today, the word *stoic* refers to people who don't show emotion. Epicureans like good food and comfort. Cynics believe that most people act out of selfishness. Skeptics are people who doubt things.

Conclusion

lexander the Great changed the world forever. There were many sides to this great man. He killed enemies by the thousands. But once the fighting was over, he was kind and generous.

He helped spread Greek culture through the lands he conquered. The Hellenistic Age was a time of great art, ideas, and science. In many ways, Alexander's achievements helped create the world we live in today.

356 B.C.	338 B.C.	336 B.C.	334 B.C.	333 B.C.	331 B.C.
Alexander is born.	Battle of Chaeronea	Alexander becomes king of Macedonia.	Alexander invades Persia; Battle of Granicus	Battle of Issus	Founding of Alexandria

TIME LINE OF ALEXANDER'S LIFE

Had Alexander lived longer, perhaps he might have come closer to making his empire one nation.

What we do know is that, more than two thousand years after his death, Alexander still fascinates and inspires us. He will always be Alexander the Great.

POINT

TALK ABOUT IT

How would you describe Alexander? What kind of person do you think he was? Share your thoughts with others who have read the book.

▲ This is a statue of Alexander.

331 B.C.	330 B.C.	324 B.C.	323 B.C.	30 B.C.
Battle of Gaugamela	Alexander becomes king of Asia.	Alexander returns.	Alexander dies. Hellenistic Age begins.	Hellenistic Age ends.

ANSWERS TO SOLVE THIS

1. Page 9 A ratio of 2 Macedonians to 1 Greek (2:1).
Math Checkpoint. Divide to solve.
Step 1: Use the data to write a ratio. 14,000/7,000
Step 2: Simplify the ratio. 14,000/7,000 = 14/7 = 2/1 or 2:1

2. Page 12 About 700 miles.
Math Checkpoint. The scale of miles is needed to solve the problem.

3. Page 14 9,000 men. 30,000 x 0.30 = 9,000
Math Checkpoint. You did not need to know the number killed.

4. Page 15 About 1,800 miles.
Math Checkpoint. The scale of miles is needed to solve the problem.

5. Page 18 The Hellenistic Age lasted 293 years. 323 − 30 = 293
Math Checkpoint. You need the dates that are given in the chapter title.

6. Page 21 The perimeter of the octagon is 480 feet. 60 x 8 = 480
Math Checkpoint. A regular octagon has 8 sides of equal length, so multiply the length of one side (60 ft) by the number of sides (8) to find the perimeter.

Glossary

ancestor	(AN-sehs-tuhr) a person in a family who lived a very long time ago (page 4)
catapult	(KAT-ah-poolt) an old war device for hurling missiles (page 10)
city-state	(SIT-ee stayt) an independent city that has its own government and controls the territory around it (page 23)
civilization	(sih-vih-lih-ZAY-shun) the culture developed by a nation or region; an advanced state of development marked by progress in the arts, sciences, and law (page 4)
classification	(klas-ih-fi-KAY-shuhn) process of grouping things or people according to similarities (page 6)
colony	(KAH-luh-nee) a land ruled by a distant country (page 7)
economy	(ee-KON-uh-mee) activity having to do with money and business (page 22)
empire	(EHM-pigh'r) a group of different lands and people governed by the same ruler (page 3)
prophecy	(PRAH-fih-see) a prediction about the future, inspired by a god (page 10)
route	(ROOT) a road or way for travel from one place to another (page 22)

Index